# PHINEHAS

## THE JAVELIN AND THE FLESH-HOOK

ERNEST HALE AKWENUKE

SYNCTERFACE™
**Syncterface Media**
London
www.syncterfacemedia.com

## PHINEHAS
### The Javelin and The Flesh-hook

ISBN: 978-1-912896-03-5
Copyright © February 2024

### Ernest Hale Akwenuke

Published in the United Kingdom by

Syncterface Media, London
*www.syncterfacemedia.com*

**Cover Design:**
Syncterface Media

*This book is printed on acid-free paper*

*To all the faithful servants of God*
*who often cry to God for a restoration*
*of His glory upon the Church of the Lord Jesus*

# FOREWORD

In this seminal and analytical work of biblical scholarship, the author, Dr Ernest Akwenuke, presents a picture of two personalities who bear the same name, share a common Levitical priestly heritage and observe liturgical and ritual ordinances in God's Temple during different epochs in the history of ancient Israel. Phinehas, the son of Eleazar, whose story is catalogued in Numbers 25, serves the God of Israel with reverence and righteous zeal. And as a reward for his loyalty and dutifulness, he obtains God's unqualified endorsement and approbation. While Phinehas, the son of Eli, whose story is rendered in 1 Samuel, dishonours God through the disrespectful and disdainful manner in which he undertakes his priestly duties in God's Temple. In consequence, he receives due reprobation and suffers rejection by God.

The author then proceeds to compare and contrast the respective attitudes and approaches of these Old Testament priests. He then goes on to identify certain parallels between them and some modern-day ministers of the gospel, ministers who function as a royal priesthood under the dispensation of the New Testament. Some of the parallels he draws are worrying and troubling. In a thought-provoking manner, he highlights some of the irreverent, indulgent and reckless excesses of some of these contemporary ministers of the gospel. With concerned and impassioned tones, he appeals to such ministers to retrace their steps and desist from drawing men unto themselves rather than unto the Lord.

The genuineness of his concerns is underscored by the fact that he conveys them without a hint of self-righteousness or a holier-than-thou attitude. He acknowledges that no human being is flawless. He is simply motivated by a sense of zealousness and a deep desire to see God's presence, power and glory restored to the Church for the benefit of the Body of Christ.

This book is timely, relevant, and challenging and will give pause for thought to Christian ministry leaders and those who aspire to such positions. It will also provide food for thought for routine readers to ruminate and reflect upon as they consider their walk with God. For Christian leaders and ministers, in particular, it will serve as a mirror by which they can examine the nature and quality of the service they offer to the Lord. Based on what they see reflected in this mirror, they can then decide which of the two *Phinehases* they presently resemble. And on the strength of their reflected observations, they can then determine whether or not a change in their approach to ministerial service is required.

Given the topicality of this book, I recommend it as essential reading to all those engaged in Christian leadership and ministerial service.

*~ Pastor Taiwo Odukoya*

# A WORD FROM THE AUTHOR

This book is an analytical interpretation of the lives and works of two priests of the Levitical Order. They shared the same name, and they were both descendants of Levi, but their response, commitment and perspective to the things of God were totally different.

Just like in the days of Nehemiah and Josiah when there was a departure from the ways of God, we need to hear the words of the book of the Lord read to us again. We need to make the necessary adjustments to make God's presence and favour come alive in our hearts and ministries once again.

*~ Ernest Hale Akwenuke*

# Contents

# PROLOGUE
## The Divine Purpose of Priesthood

*⁹ But you are a chosen people, a royal priesthood, a holy nation, God's special possession, that you may declare the praises of him who called you out of darkness into his wonderful light.*

~ 1 Peter 2:9 (NIV)

From this scripture, it is clear that all who have become God's possession belong to the New Testament body of priests. Whereas in the Old Testament, only the Levites were called to be priests, this grace has been accorded to all of us who are in Christ in the New Testament.

This volume is for the benefit of those called into this New Testament company of priests. As the Good

Book says in 1 Corinthians:

> ¹¹ *These things happened to them as examples and were written down as warnings for us, on whom the culmination of the ages has come.*
>
> ~ 1 Corinthians 10:11 (NIV)

# FAILURE:
## Man's Default Position

Without controversy, we have failed God and disappointed Him so many times by the errant ways we have walked since coming to know Him. We have walked in disobedience, placing our own will before His. We have not given God His due *(They say unto him, Caesar's. Then saith he unto them, Render therefore unto Caesar the things which are Caesar's; and unto God the things that are God's ~ Matthew 22:21)*, and we have not diligently pursued His purposes as set out in the Word and impressed upon our spirits. In truth, and as the scripture attests, *"We all, like sheep, have gone astray, each of us has turned to our own way; and the Lord has laid on him the iniquity of us all."* (Isaiah 53:6).

From the scriptures, we also see and recognise that

*"If we claim to be without sin, we deceive ourselves and the truth is not in us."* (1 John 1:8).

Indeed, so reprehensible are our ways that if told, some friends and acquaintances might deny us, that is until their scandalous ways are turned over and also exposed.

Most of us have experienced the powerlessness of our efforts when striving against sin. Borrowing the fig leaves from Adam, we seek ways and means to hide our sins in our bosom *(Job 31:33 - If I covered my transgressions as Adam, by hiding mine iniquity in my bosom)*. Like Achan, we have cherished and hidden the accursed things in our secret places to the detriment and harm of ourselves, our spiritual and natural children, fellow church members, prayer partners, co-leaders, committee members and others around us.

Alas, it seems our cries are no longer heard on high. Painfully the hearts of many have followed other gods in search of deliverance. Because all have sinned and fallen short of experiencing the manifest glory of God, we have become like people who have no God, and unfortunately, there are only a handful of priests to read us the word of the Lord.

The priests and ministers of the Lord are the head of the flock. They are, therefore, the primary target of the enemy, for compromising the priesthood is the surest way to scatter the flock and decimate God's people.

*⁷ Awake, O sword, against my shepherd, and against the man that is my fellow, saith the Lord of hosts: smite the shepherd, and the sheep shall be scattered: and I will turn mine hand upon the little ones.*

~ Zechariah 13:7

Has the enemy of our souls not made good progress in this regard? However, thank God, Jesus has been smitten for us so that as under-shepherds, we now have protection from being smitten! Many of our pulpits have ceased to declare the wholesome words of our Lord Jesus Christ. Instead, they share sound bites of distorted scripture to energise people to do their bidding and not the Lord's. This should vex the soul of anyone who desires righteousness, peace and joy in our Christian and broader communities, attributes that indicate the entrance of the Kingdom of our God into our communal lives. As it is written, *"For the kingdom of God is not meat and drink; but righteousness, and peace, and joy in the Holy Ghost."* (Romans 14:17)

"Thank God, Jesus has been smitten for us so that as under-shepherds, we now have protection from being smitten!"

# PHINEHAS:
## Two Priests Serving Opposing Kingdoms

In the book of Numbers 25, Phinehas was the son of Eleazar, the grandson of Aaron, Moses' brother. So, Moses, the great prophet and leader of the Israelites, was Phinehas' great uncle. We must also not forget that Phinehas' father Eleazar was a high priest of God, just like Aaron. Thus, there is no doubt that this fellow came from a very reputable spiritual background. It would, therefore, be safe to assume that he was well taught, by precept and, of course, example, to walk in the way of the God of his fathers.

Phinehas had been taught the benefits of walking the path of God and had seen the consequences of failure to walk the righteous path. He had seen the saints faint, fail and fall for not walking the path. He had seen the nation of God's people suffer needlessly in the wilderness for choosing not to walk the path of God's Word and ordinance. On the other hand, he had also witnessed the great deliverances of the Lord, the manifestations of God's power and grace, and the execution of His authority. Phinehas had come to know the goodness and severity of God, and he also knew which of these two attributes of God's persona he would rather experience.

Like us, Phinehas, son of Eleazar, lived among folks who chose their own way above the way of the Lord. So, he had every opportunity to join the crowd, but his choice was most likely influenced by both his commitment to God and his pedigree. He chose to fight the Lord's corner, executing the Lord's judgement.

Then there was another Phinehas who came along. We read about him in the book of 1 Samuel 1 until his demise in chapter 4 of the same book. This Phinehas was also of priestly lineage; he was one of the sons of Eli, the high priest. Possibly the intention was for him to someday take over the reins of the high priesthood from his father, Eli. Sadly, he did not have the same heart as the son of Eleazar. He was bereft of zeal and a desire to please God. He was not only self-indulgent and complacent about growth in the ministry; he actively lured and urged God's people to follow suit and to disregard the things of God and the fear of the Lord.

This Phinehas lived without the fear of God. Openly within the forecourts of the temple, he disdained the sacrifice by polluting it and those that brought it. Along with his brother Hophni, he shunned the voice of correction and became both profligate and reprobate. Phinehas demonstrated his reprobate mind by going to war with the armies of the Lord, whom he had despised repeatedly. So, it comes as no surprise that the Lord rejected him and no longer acknowledged him. The signification of the Holy Ghost is that there are many Phinehases today who despise the Kingdom they step forward to represent. Unlike the first Phinehas, they have fallen out of faith.

Now the word of God describes us as a royal priesthood. The question is, which Phinehas does our priesthood identify with? Which Phinehas do we copy or appear to mimic in our ministry and our Christian service?

"Which Phinehas do we copy or appear to mimic in our ministry and Christian service?"

## THE BURDEN AND WORKS OF
## PHINEHAS, SON OF ELEAZAR

Phinehas, son of Eleazar, was immensely committed to God and His ways. Watching his people depart from God and reap the horrendous fruit of death saddened him. The wages of sin have always been and still is death, and his people were reaping from what they had sowed. He was so sad that he felt the need to act.

Note that whatever action or inaction you choose will place you in the same position as, or in alignment with, either Phinehas, the son of Eleazar or Phinehas, the son of Eli.

The action Phinehas, son of Eleazar, took at a time when God's people were going astray was what made God approve and endorse him.

⁶ And, behold, one of the children of Israel came and brought unto his brethren a Midianitish woman in the sight of Moses, and in the sight of all the congregation of the children of Israel, who were weeping before the door of the tabernacle of the congregation.

⁷ And when Phinehas, the son of Eleazar, the son of Aaron the priest, saw it, he rose up from among the congregation, and took a javelin in his hand;

⁸ And he went after the man of Israel into the tent, and thrust both of them through, the man of Israel, and the woman through her belly. So the plague was stayed from the children of Israel.

⁹ And those that died in the plague were twenty and four thousand.

¹⁰ And the Lord spake unto Moses, saying,

¹¹ Phinehas, the son of Eleazar, the son of Aaron the priest, hath turned my wrath away from the children of Israel, while he was zealous for my sake among them, that I consumed not the children of Israel in my jealousy.

¹² Wherefore say, Behold, I give unto him my covenant of peace:

¹³ And he shall have it, and his seed after him, even the covenant of an everlasting priesthood; because he was zealous for his God, and made an atonement for the children of Israel.

¹⁴ Now the name of the Israelite that was slain, even that was slain with the Midianitish woman, was Zimri, the son of Salu, a prince of a chief house among the Simeonites.

¹⁵ And the name of the Midianitish woman that was slain was Cozbi, the daughter of Zur; he was head over a people, and of a chief house in Midian.

~ Numbers 25:6-15

From this passage of scripture, we see how righteously indignant Phinehas became over the lack of the fear of God displayed by Zimri. Zimri, a child of Israel, carried himself with cocky arrogance and without fear, even in the presence of the Lord. He showed no reverence whatsoever. The people were weeping before the Lord, and he sauntered in with his prized possession, his trophy mistress, with total disregard for the Lord. Maybe Zimri thought his status as a prince of a chief house gave him the impetus to do as he desired, but our God is no respecter of persons.

Sadly, our churches have become known to harbour people like Zimri. Some have become chief men, holding key positions among the people of God, and it goes without saying that with these folks, God is not pleased. Just as this 'Zimri' attitude brought a plague upon the children of Israel, causing the death of twenty-four thousand of them, our attitude today has brought a plague of darkness upon us that has hidden the light of God's life from us. As a result, the sinners we ought to be a guiding light to are dying in ignorance, without eternal hope. The glory is hidden from us, and we tremble with fear before our enemies and those who contend with us, thereby living short of the provision of the scripture that says:

> [25] *But this is what the Lord says: "Yes, captives will be taken from warriors, and plunder retrieved from the fierce; I will contend with those who contend with you, and your children I will save.*
>
> ~ Isaiah 49:25 (NIV)

13

*¹² Though you search for your enemies, you will not find them. Those who wage war against you will be as nothing at all.*

~ Isaiah 41:12 (NIV)

From these scriptures, we see what happens when we have God on our side. However, with the wrong attitude and without God on our side to fight on our behalf, many tend to seek other means of deliverance even though they are churchgoers and profess Christianity.

In the early nineteen nineties, I was invited to minister at a church. Before the meeting, I had pleaded with God to help me see over the wall, to give me a glimpse into hidden and unknown things and give me insight into what He wished to do at the meeting. God showed me a man wearing a whitish French suit standing to the left of the pulpit. The Lord told me that the man had been visiting a voodoo priest or witch doctor, as well as attending church. I was shocked as I thought it impossible at that time. But surely, just as God had shown me, this chap was present at the meeting, and he stepped forward for help.

Today, what seemed so farfetched back then is much more prevalent. There seem to be many more like the man in the French suit in our churches; those who resort to self-help alternatives with dire eternal consequences simply because they do not see the power and presence of the Godhead on our pulpits. Some folks manufacture inexistent scriptures such as "heaven helps those who help themselves" to justify their departure from the wholesome words of our Lord Jesus Christ.

During a trip to the Republic of Haiti, I was told that the country was ninety per cent Catholic and a hundred per cent voodoo. Sad as that may sound, we must withstand and resist the onslaught of these servants of the enemy who have crept in among us if we do not want our Christianity described in the same way.

Unlike Phinehas, the son of Eleazar, who responded to prevent the fall of his people from grace into the abyss of God's rejection, Phinehas, the son of Eli, let things drift. He not only endorsed sin, but he also chose not to listen to anyone who sought to correct him, including his father and went ahead to exemplify the practice of sin;

> [30] *Therefore Jehovah, the God of Israel, saith, I said indeed that thy house, and the house of thy father, should walk before me for ever: but now Jehovah saith, Be it far from me; for them that honor me I will honor, and they that despise me shall be lightly esteemed.*
> ~ 1 Samuel 2:30 (ASV).

The above scripture warns of how God can change His mind regarding anyone who persistently ignores His counsel. We also see the importance of honouring the Lord with our lives and ministries. As the sons of Eli did, failure to honour God reduces a man and his ministry to one lowly esteemed by Jehovah.

Today we contend with this same 'son of Eli' attitude

to ministry. Some ministers of the new covenant simply look the other way and tacitly endorse sin to keep the floods of people and their substance coming through the church doors while shutting out the Head of the Church, the Son of God Himself. Some may have even gone beyond endorsing sin to encouraging people through the distortion of the holy writ to practise sin. They preach on every subject save on the wages of sin. They encourage folk to believe God for everything God's grace has to offer, except the grace to lay aside the so easily besetting sin. They have moved from the acceptable by God to the acceptable by men, thereby becoming one of many teachers heaped up by those who do not endure sound doctrine, having itching ears.

> [3] *For the time will come when they will not endure sound doctrine; but after their own lusts shall they heap to themselves teachers, having itching ears;*
>
> ~ 2 Timothy 4:3

## The Goodness and Severity of God

Falling from the place of grace tends to attract the severity of God. Many of us wish to enjoy God's goodness despite walking away from His grace. So often, we want to stroll into His presence while bearing the trophies of our lust. We ignore the pain and weeping of saints around us and persist willfully and selfishly in our error in the church, among God's people and in the presence of Him from whom nothing is hidden. Zimri failed to understand the goodness and severity of the Lord.

Now take a look at this:

> [20] *Well; because of unbelief they were broken off, and thou standest by faith. Be not highminded, but fear:*
> [21] *For if God spared not the natural branches, take heed lest he also spare not thee.*
> [22] *Behold therefore the goodness and severity of God: on them which fell, severity; but toward thee, goodness, if thou continue in his goodness: otherwise thou also shalt be cut off.*
>
> ~ Romans 11:20-22

## "Key Man" Attitude

Zimri was of the stock of key men, and so was Cozbi, his Midianitish consort. Some men have been blessed or appear so to be, and as a result, assume key positions in our communities, including the church. For the simple reason that spending time with God has been forsaken by these, they forget the source of their blessings and gifts and drift into the 'grey area' of living in darkness while reminiscing on the residual light of their past glorious experiences of God; an area where sin is appealing, not repented of and where God does not reside. In many cases, when we find ourselves in this position, and I have been there, we make excuses and still expect God to show up when we want Him to. We expect God to move the goalposts for us because of His grace; we simply want the best of both worlds! This was the attitude characterised and epitomised by Zimri's behaviour.

Zimri wanted to keep his trophy, the Midianitish woman, and still partake with the congregation of

God's people, something quite common in this day and age. We want to keep our trophies of lust, power and influence yet fellowship with the people of God in His presence. Now imagine if Zimri got away with it. Suddenly it would have become free for all among the children of Israel. They would have gone ahead and fulfilled their highest lustful wishes and desires, despite God's disapproval, fearlessly parading themselves before His presence. God, the jealous One, would have been relegated to the bottom of the priority list of the children of Israel, whom He had so mightily rescued from Pharaoh and his army. Then the Lord God would have had to leave them. This was what Phinehas, the son of Eleazer, dreaded and why he took prompt and decisive action against Zimri.

## Challenging the "Key Man" Attitude

In both testaments, we see that God's Word and ordinances are preeminent and that all men are subject to His Word. We have read about how Phinehas, the son of Eleazar, challenged and took out Zimri and Cozbi, children of key families amongst their people. We also see how Paul rebukes Peter in the book of Galatians over his attitude towards the Gentile believers.

Nowadays, traditional, religious and sense knowledge belief systems seem to negate or perhaps supersede the examples and commandments in the Word. The scripture declares, *"Rebuke not an elder, but intreat him as a father;"* (1 Timothy 5:1). The representative word here is elder. A member of the church leadership or council with responsibility for the souls of the flock; not a top donor who, on account of his donations to the church, in some cases from ill-gotten gain, assumes he is at liberty and has the right to defy God and His Word without bearing the consequences. Indeed, sinners are welcome to join the congregation of the righteous, not to sow evil seeds to turn God's people back to living in sin, but rather to be converted from their sins and follow God.

However, sinners who glory in their sin and seek to intimidate saints with ill-gotten gain or contemporary ideologies that negate and undermine scripture, leaving their ungodly mark in the church by defiling our women and stirring unholy passions among our men are not welcome. They must not be allowed to address the congregation of the righteous either. There is no precedence in scripture, neither is there a place in these end times for such unscriptural practices. We are admonished to take heed of what we hear. Therefore, the culture of handing microphones to ungodly key men and entertainers who come to church meetings to speak words that either oppose the teachings of Christ or fall short of edifying the saints must be rejected and shunned by God's servants and people. One might say, "He is a key man; you cannot say 'NO' to him." Well, this will come as bad news to the Zimrites; simply tell them that Eleazar's son, Phinehas, just came to town!

God is raising a people who will thrust the Word at those who imagine they can exalt themselves above Him. Not in fear, but in love and in the spirit of meekness coupled with the favour of God, to turn many back again to the path of righteousness and true fellowship with Him. Then will the saints thrive and live as the salt and light that preserves and guides the world around us, for this is the role ordained for the saints. This will halt the plagues of spiritual death, economic deprivation and hopelessness in our society as accountability becomes restored to our civil society because the saints declare the Truth from the housetops, and it is echoed along our streets, becoming the standard in our land! This was what John the Baptist did in his day to usher in our Lord Jesus, and it is what we must do in our day, stirring ourselves into action and hastening the coming of the Lord.

# THE PLAGUE OF SPIRITUAL DEATH

F ast forward in time to the day of Eli. Phinehas, the son of Eleazer, is now dead, and unsurprisingly the children of Israel are at a crossroads once again. Eli, the high priest at the time, had aptly named one of his sons Phinehas, possibly hoping that he will grow up to be the arrowhead of God. Not so! Phinehas joined the bandwagon, or perhaps one should say he co-initiated the bandwagon of decline to wanton trophy hunting and its ostentatious display among God's people. From scripture, we see that Eli essentially paved the way for this:

> [27] *And there came a man of God unto Eli, and said unto him, Thus saith the Lord, Did I plainly appear unto the house of thy father, when they were in Egypt in Pharaoh's house?*

*²⁸ And did I choose him out of all the tribes of Israel to be my priest, to offer upon mine altar, to burn incense, to wear an ephod before me? And did I give unto the house of thy father all the offerings made by fire of the children of Israel?*
*²⁹ Wherefore kick ye at my sacrifice and at mine offering, which I have commanded in my habitation; and honourest thy sons above me, to make yourselves fat with the chiefest of all the offerings of Israel my people?*
~ 1 Samuel 2:27-29

Phinehas, Eli's son, was not satisfied with his position as a priest. He was lustful and not content with what he was entitled to by the ordinance regarding offerings to God by the people. He wanted part of God's share, and he also wanted the women who brought the offerings. This was no doubt a slippery, downward slope.

The Bible says, *"godliness with contentment is great gain"* (1 Timothy 6:6), and that *"holding faith, and a good conscience; which some having put away concerning faith have made shipwreck"* (1 Timothy 1:19). Once Phinehas lost contentment, he also lost his grip on faith and a good conscience and headed for big trouble. He began to reach out to the things that belonged to God and defiled himself, his calling, his priesthood. His offering became abominable.

The three-pronged flesh-hook, an instrument reserved for service at the altar of God, found its way outside the tabernacle to the common areas where the sinners were, to serve the purposes of Phinehas' greed. This three-pronged instrument that was supposed to be a symbol of righteousness, peace and joy in the Holy Ghost to Phinehas became an instrument of self-service; the lust of the flesh, the lust of the eyes and the pride of life. Instead of walking in righteousness, with peace and joy, and serving the Lord, he opted for self-gratification in the lust of his eyes and flesh with pride, serving himself and, by implication, serving and glorifying the devil.

This son of a high priest represents another class of priests. A group that puts self first, instead of the Kingdom. Rather than serve the people, the people serve them and their lusts. They do not eagerly point the people to the Light and the Light alone. Instead, they stand in the limelight and pretend to speak of the Lord as the Light, deceiving the simple-minded who see them as their lord and follow them with unquestioning commitment. Some of their followers even go to ungodly lengths to gain their endorsement, like those who were led astray by Phinehas, the son of Eli, in the book of 1 Samuel 2: 15-16:

> [15] *Also before they burnt the fat, the priest's servant came, and said to the man that sacrificed, Give flesh to roast for the priest; for he will not have sodden flesh of thee, but raw.*
> [16] *And if any man said unto him, Let them not fail to burn the fat presently, and then take as much as thy soul desireth; then he would answer him, Nay; but thou shalt give it me now: and if not, I will take it by force.*

Another disturbing characteristic of this type of

priest is that they disregard God's opinion about their works and carry on as though God is well pleased with them. These presumptuous and self-willed ones are described as spots among us, and like the son of Eli, they join themselves with the armies of the cross only to bring about shame and defeat in our battle against the cohorts of hell. These, just like Phinehas, the son of Eli, are the progenitors of the departure of the glory we once enjoyed in our communion with God, for when this Phinehas had a child, the child was appropriately called Ichabod - the glory has departed.

People of God, we must act fast and without fear. Resist the sons of Eli and thrust the Word at the Zimrites that seek to attend, participate in, and defile our holy blood, bought and preserved convocations.

# THE THREE-PRONGED FLESH-HOOK

The verses below are an apt description of this day and age. They show us where we are right now regarding the priests, ministers, teachers, prophets and pastors of our day.

13 *And the priest's custom with the people was, that, when any man offered sacrifice, the priest's servant came, while the flesh was in seething, with a flesh-hook of three teeth in his hand;*

14 *And he struck it into the pan, or kettle, or caldron, or pot; all that the flesh-hook brought up the priest took for himself. So they did in Shiloh unto all the Israelites that came thither.*

15 *Also before they burnt the fat, the priest's servant came, and said to the man that sacrificed, Give flesh to roast for the priest; for he will not have sodden flesh of*

*thee, but raw.*

*¹⁶ And if any man said unto him, Let them not fail to burn the fat presently, and then take as much as thy soul desireth; then he would answer him, Nay; but thou shalt give it me now: and if not, I will take it by force.*

*¹⁷ Wherefore the sin of the young men was very great before the Lord: for men abhorred the offering of the Lord.*

~ 1 Samuel 2:13-17

*¹ And I said, Hear, I pray you, O heads of Jacob, and ye princes of the house of Israel; Is it not for you to know judgment?*

*² Who hate the good, and love the evil; who pluck off their skin from off them, and their flesh from off their bones;*

*³ Who also eat the flesh of my people, and flay their skin from off them; and they break their bones, and chop them in pieces, as for the pot, and as flesh within the caldron.*

*⁴ Then shall they cry unto the Lord, but he will not hear them: he will even hide his face from them at that time, as they have behaved themselves ill in their doings.*

*⁵ Thus saith the Lord concerning the prophets that make my people err, that bite with their teeth, and cry, Peace; and he that putteth not into their mouths, they even prepare war against him.*

*⁶ Therefore night shall be unto you, that ye shall not have a vision; and it shall be dark unto you, that ye shall not divine; and the sun shall go down over the prophets, and the day shall be dark over them.*

*⁷ Then shall the seers be ashamed, and the diviners confounded: yea, they shall all cover their lips; for there is no answer of God.*

*⁸ But truly I am full of power by the spirit of the Lord, and of judgment, and of might, to declare unto Jacob his transgression, and to Israel his sin.*

*⁹ Hear this, I pray you, ye heads of the house of Jacob, and princes of the house of Israel, that abhor judgment, and pervert all equity.*

*¹⁰ They build up Zion with blood, and Jerusalem with iniquity.*

*¹¹ The heads thereof judge for reward, and the priests thereof teach for hire, and the prophets thereof divine for money: yet will they lean upon the Lord, and say, Is not the Lord among us? none evil can come upon us.*

~ Micah 3:1-11

These verses highlight the tragedy that has befallen the Church. The tragedy of Micah's day, which is notable in verses 5b and 11, is all too familiar when comparing it to what we contend with today. The enterprise of money has blighted the ministry and service of the Lord and the people. But I rejoice because there is nothing impossible with our God. He is a restorer; He is a repairer of the breach.

So, let us look at the similarities between Phinehas', the son of Eli's ministry and what is prevalent in the church today. The book of Numbers 4 reads:

*¹³ And they shall take away the ashes from the altar, and spread a purple cloth thereon:*

*¹⁴ And they shall put upon it all the vessels thereof, wherewith they minister about it, even the censers, the flesh-hooks, and the shovels, and the basons, all the vessels of the altar; and they shall spread upon it a covering of badgers' skins, and put to the staves of it.*

Here, we see the flesh-hook as an instrument of service used at the altar. However, from the scripture we read earlier, during Phinehas son of Eli's time, this was not the purpose of the flesh-hook. The flesh-hook was no longer used exclusively at the altar. Instead, it was used to serve Phinehas' purposes, used to retrieve the sacrifice of the people from their cauldrons. This sacred tool of service was now being handled by Phinehas' servants to achieve personal, ungodly desires. Notice what the scripture says in verse 15:

> *15 And when Aaron and his sons have made an end of covering the sanctuary, and all the vessels of the sanctuary, as the camp is to set forward; after that, the sons of Kohath shall come to bear it: but they shall not touch any holy thing, lest they die. These things are the burden of the sons of Kohath in the tabernacle of the congregation.*
>
> ~ Numbers 4:15

Here, even the carriers of these holy instruments had to be careful not to touch any holy thing, yet Phinehas brazenly ordered his servants to use the holy tools to fulfil his lust. I am almost certain that these servants would have used this trick for their own gain as well. Decadence! They were tinkering with death, spiritual death.

We hear of people who have served apprenticeships in these ungodly son of Eli establishments; how they rise and serve themselves in their own churches, which are fashioned after the pattern they served under. Their drive is not the people's emancipation but theirs. They simply carry the ill practices they learnt during their stewardship into their new setup. There is, therefore, a proliferation of this "son of Eli" type of ministries across the land. There is also an increase in the number of entities with "Ichabod'"spiritually inscribed on their doorposts.

We understand from God's word that He disapproves of marriages and affiliations with those outside His kingdom. The reason is simply that like begets like, hence resulting in the pollution of His people. In the same vein, when these son of Eli ministries choose demonic doctrines, their spiritual seed can only be a product of their waywardness. God's word makes it clear that a good tree cannot bear bad fruit, and an evil tree cannot bear good fruit. This explains the replication process of these ministries that do not uphold God's word: They were simply not born of the Word!

> *8 Bring forth therefore fruits meet for repentance:*
> *9 And think not to say within yourselves, We have Abraham to our father: for I say unto you, that God is able of these stones to raise up children unto Abraham.*
> *10 And now also the axe is laid unto the root of the trees: therefore every tree which bringeth not forth good fruit is hewn down, and cast into the fire.*
>
> ·· Matthew 3:8-10

God demands that we turn around and bring forth fruit befitting of those whose hearts He has touched.

We cannot coast on the grace granted to mankind. We must follow through with the teaching of that grace.

> *11 For the grace of God that bringeth salvation hath appeared to all men,*
> *12 Teaching us that, denying ungodliness and worldly lusts, we should live soberly, righteously, and godly, in this present world;*
>
> ~ Titus 2:11-12

We must assume our place; the place bequeathed us by the Word that "God is able of these stones to raise up children unto Abraham". We are those stones raised to life through our identification with the resurrection of our Lord Jesus.

> *5 Ye also, as lively stones, are built up a spiritual house, an holy priesthood, to offer up spiritual sacrifices, acceptable to God by Jesus Christ.*
>
> ~ 1 Peter 2:5

This is the calibre of priesthood that God is looking for, the calibre of priesthood He desires to serve Him. We must return to the standard of the Word. We must eschew doctrines of men, and more so of demons that have crept in unawares and taken a grip on the Church.

I remember meeting a voodoo pastor in London, England, back in 2012. He told me that he had dreamt about me, and in the dream, he had given me a special power. This pastor then urged me to buy his books, read them and advised me to attend his services. This would have enabled the transfer of his evil power to me as I would be sitting directly under his ministry. Thank God I did not fall for that evil deceit. However, it goes to demonstrate that as children of the Most High, we need to be careful who we listen to. As the scripture says in Mark 4:24, "take heed what you hear..." because there is a high possibility that there will be a transfer of that spirit to you. We must, therefore, uphold the Word as our standard, and we must forcefully reject anything that falls short of this standard.

During some of this voodoo pastor's meetings, I later learned that he asked his parishioners to draw a caricature of whoever they perceived to be an enemy. He then told them to stab the caricature, rip the sheet of paper, and finally discard it at a three-way junction or in a flowing stream. Parishioners were also encouraged to bring knives to these prayer meetings to carry out this act. Apart from all that, he also sold them salt to sprinkle around their homes to protect them from evil spirits. Whatever happened to the eternal, unchanging, all-powerful blood of Jesus Christ?

So be wary of imposters, those who claim to be givers of special powers. They are like the sons of Belial laying claim to the power endowing work of the divine Spirit of grace, thus trying to render the Holy Ghost ineffective.

There is an endless range of false teachings and practices. While godly leaders must be bold enough to walk away from anything that has no basis in scripture, irrespective of how consistent and reliable it appears to be, parishioners and church members must be brave enough to ask their leaders, without any hint of arrogance, to clarify from scripture anything that they are unsure of. More importantly, they should be able to study the scripture and see for themselves if it is so.

Anything not based on the Word cannot and will not bring about life, deliverance or salvation. So, offering anything but the Word to God's people will not transform stones into lively stones even with the best of intentions. This can only be done by our Lord through His Word. We must return to the teaching of the scriptures. Only then will we see God at work again. Remember, there is no substitute for the Word of life.

There was a time, not too long ago, when some prophets were reporting a plethora of visitations of Jesus. There were claims of this Jesus telling them things that were not scriptural. I remember objecting to some of the claims of one of these so-called prophets whose revelation was published on social media. I encouraged his followers to study the scriptures to see if these words were true, like the Bereans in the book of Acts. However, I was reprimanded by a sincere and zealous but misguided Christian brother that it made no sense judging these so-called revelations by the scriptures because, in his words, 'these are perilous times, not Berean times'. It was shocking to hear someone suggest that scrutiny by the Word is time or period dependent!

At no time or period in man's history can departing from the scripture be acceptable or justifiable. The Word must remain our standard till Jesus appears, and we are changed to His likeness completing the work of the Word, which transforms our lives daily. Amen!

---

"Our attitude today has brought a plague of darkness upon us that has hidden the light of God's life from us"

---

# TWO KINDS OF PRIESTHOODS

[1] *On that day the Book of Moses was read aloud in the hearing of the people and there it was found written that no Ammonite or Moabite should ever be admitted into the assembly of God,*

[2] *because they had not met the Israelites with food and water but had hired Balaam to call a curse down on them. (Our God, however, turned the curse into a blessing.)*

[3] *When the people heard this law, they excluded from Israel all who were of foreign descent.*

[4] *Before this, Eliashib the priest had been put in charge of the storerooms of the house of our God. He was closely associated with Tobiah,*

[5] *and he had provided him with a large room formerly used to store the grain offerings and incense and temple articles, and also the tithes of grain, new wine and olive oil prescribed for the Levites, musicians and*

gatekeepers, as well as the contributions for the priests.
⁶ But while all this was going on, I was not in Jerusalem, for in the thirty-second year of Artaxerxes king of Babylon I had returned to the king. Some time later I asked his permission
⁷ and came back to Jerusalem. Here I learned about the evil thing Eliashib had done in providing Tobiah a room in the courts of the house of God.
⁸ I was greatly displeased and threw all Tobiah's household goods out of the room.
⁹ I gave orders to purify the rooms, and then I put back into them the equipment of the house of God, with the grain offerings and the incense.
¹⁰ I also learned that the portions assigned to the Levites had not been given to them, and that all the Levites and musicians responsible for the service had gone back to their own fields.
¹¹ So I rebuked the officials and asked them, "Why is the house of God neglected?" Then I called them together and stationed them at their posts.
¹² All Judah brought the tithes of grain, new wine and olive oil into the storerooms.
¹³ I put Shelemiah the priest, Zadok the scribe, and a Levite named Pedaiah in charge of the storerooms and made Hanan son of Zakkur, the son of Mattaniah, their assistant, because they were considered trustworthy. They were made responsible for distributing the supplies to their fellow Levites.
¹⁴ Remember me for this, my God, and do not blot out what I have so faithfully done for the house of my God and its services.
¹⁵ In those days I saw people in Judah treading winepresses on the Sabbath and bringing in grain and loading it on donkeys, together with wine, grapes, figs

and all other kinds of loads. And they were bringing all this into Jerusalem on the Sabbath. Therefore I warned them against selling food on that day.

¹⁶ People from Tyre who lived in Jerusalem were bringing in fish and all kinds of merchandise and selling them in Jerusalem on the Sabbath to the people of Judah.

¹⁷ I rebuked the nobles of Judah and said to them, "What is this wicked thing you are doing – desecrating the Sabbath day?

¹⁸ Didn't your ancestors do the same things, so that our God brought all this calamity on us and on this city? Now you are stirring up more wrath against Israel by desecrating the Sabbath."

¹⁹ When evening shadows fell on the gates of Jerusalem before the Sabbath, I ordered the doors to be shut and not opened until the Sabbath was over. I stationed some of my own men at the gates so that no load could be brought in on the Sabbath day.

²⁰ Once or twice the merchants and sellers of all kinds of goods spent the night outside Jerusalem.

²¹ But I warned them and said, "Why do you spend the night by the wall? If you do this again, I will arrest you." From that time on they no longer came on the Sabbath.

²² Then I commanded the Levites to purify themselves and go and guard the gates in order to keep the Sabbath day holy. Remember me for this also, my God, and show mercy to me according to your great love.

²³ Moreover, in those days I saw men of Judah who had married women from Ashdod, Ammon and Moab.

²⁴ Half of their children spoke the language of Ashdod or the language of one of the other peoples, and did not know how to speak the language of Judah.

²⁵ I rebuked them and called curses down on them. I beat

*some of the men and pulled out their hair. I made them take an oath in God's name and said: "You are not to give your daughters in marriage to their sons, nor are you to take their daughters in marriage for your sons or for yourselves.*

*²⁶ Was it not because of marriages like these that Solomon king of Israel sinned? Among the many nations there was no king like him. He was loved by his God, and God made him king over all Israel, but even he was led into sin by foreign women.*

*²⁷ Must we hear now that you too are doing all this terrible wickedness and are being unfaithful to our God by marrying foreign women?"*

*²⁸ One of the sons of Joiada son of Eliashib the high priest was son-in-law to Sanballat the Horonite. And I drove him away from me.*

*²⁹ Remember them, my God, because they defiled the priestly office and the covenant of the priesthood and of the Levites.*

*³⁰ So I purified the priests and the Levites of everything foreign, and assigned them duties, each to his own task.*

*³¹ I also made provision for contributions of wood at designated times, and for the firstfruits. Remember me with favor, my God.*

~ Nehemiah 13:1-31 (NIV)

This scripture addresses some salient issues and examples of the two kinds of priesthoods we have portrayed so far. We see the spiritually destitute priest Eliashib demonstrating the very essence of Phinehas, son of Eli, type priesthood by putting his selfish motives before the Lord's. In the New Testament, he would have fallen within the category of those that Apostle Paul described in the book of Philippians 2:

> [21] *For all seek their own, not the things which are Jesus Christ's.*
>
> ~ Philippians 2:21

Eliashib started well. He worked with Nehemiah from the outset. Nehemiah saw Eliashib fit to oversee the place of worship and manage the temple. He was the high priest of God, but when the sons of Belial, Sanballat and Tobiah enticed him, he forsook the injunction given in Proverbs 1:10: *"My son if sinners entice you, do not consent"*.

In the same manner, many high priests, or big-time ministers of our day, have forsaken the eternal Word of God and discarded the scripturally prescribed manner of serving the Lord. They have replaced God's eternal and unfailing Word with the teachings and representations of devils. They serve the devil by installing imaginations of their warped portrayal of the Lord in the minds of their congregation. They instil a mindset, other than the mind of Christ, in God's people. They no longer serve the Master, Jesus, but serve another whom they have willfully chosen.

We observe that Eliashib removed the instruments of God's worship and dismissed the people anointed of God to serve. In their place, he brought in Tobiah to occupy the vacant room. Tobiah was the devil's ally, an opponent of the plans and purposes of God. This high priest exchanged the things and people of God for the things and a servant of satan. This is an antichrist spirit that has become prevalent in our day.

The proponents of this culture of disservice to God tend to dismiss people who insist on the standard of the Word and set in place paraphernalia of ungodly worship that serve their own agenda. They replace the Word with their practices and replace anointed servants of God with corrupt people and yes-men who have neither love nor a fear of God. People who practise various forms of curious arts while invoking the name of Christ.

Furthermore, there is a disturbing trend nowadays that Eliashib, the high priest of the son of Eli mould, gave assent to; the freedom of covenant association with those not born of Christ! The fruits of such associations hardly ever speak the language of God because they are not birthed by the Word. Though the offsprings of such unions may seem to speak the language of the Word, aptly referred to as 'Christianese', we know they still possess un-regenerated hearts because no one comes to Jesus except the Father draws them. Therefore, priests who use occult powers to populate their churches raise offsprings for the devil, not the Lord. This ungodly pattern is spoken about in the book of Hosea:

> [8] *"Ephraim has mixed himself among the peoples; Ephraim is a cake unturned.*
> [9] *Aliens have devoured his strength, But he does not know it; Yes, gray hairs are here and there on him, Yet he does not know it.*
> [10] *And the pride of Israel testifies to his face, But they*

*do not return to the Lord their God, Nor seek Him for all this."*

~ Hosea 7:8-10 (NKJV)

In the same manner, priests who avoid preaching the wholesome word of God to boost their congregation numbers will soon find out that their Church is made up of half-baked cakes, an offering which, based on the Word, is unlikely to be endorsed or accepted by Christ. The result of this influx of unregenerate aliens is a depletion of anointing, strength and power in the Church and among God's people.

Let us review the work of Nehemiah as an example of a priest of the Phinehas "son of Eleazar" mould. In chapter 5, we observe that he rejects the benefits of the governorship to avoid burdening the people:

*<sup>14</sup> Moreover from the time that I was appointed to be their governor in the land of Judah, from the twentieth year even unto the two and thirtieth year of Artaxerxes the king, that is, twelve years, I and my brethren have not eaten the bread of the governor.*
*<sup>15</sup> But the former governors that had been before me were chargeable unto the people, and had taken of them bread and wine, beside forty shekels of silver; yea, even their servants bare rule over the people: but so did not I, because of the fear of God.*

~ Nehemiah 5:14-15

This is what some of the current crop of leaders would rather wish was not written. Rather than follow this leadership style of tending and putting the interest of the flock first, they flay the flock like the son of Eli. As Micah laments, they make war with those that do not put into their mouths. They squeeze God's people of all their substance, spiritual and material, making themselves fat, while the flock remains lean from spiritual malnourishment. The ultimate result of this form of religion is the departure of the glory as the people murmur and complain, grieving the Holy Spirit.

Which priest will follow the paths of Phinehas, the son of Eleazar, and Nehemiah so that God will remember us for good by releasing His glory upon us? Which priest will return to the Lord his God to seek Him?

# PASTORS WHOSE MOUTHS
# MUST BE SHUT

[5] *For this cause left I thee in Crete, that thou shouldest set in order the things that are wanting, and ordain elders in every city, as I had appointed thee:*

[6] *If any be blameless, the husband of one wife, having faithful children not accused of riot or unruly.*

[7] *For a bishop must be blameless, as the steward of God; not selfwilled, not soon angry, not given to wine, no striker, not given to filthy lucre;*

[8] *But a lover of hospitality, a lover of good men, sober, just, holy, temperate;*

[9] *Holding fast the faithful word as he hath been taught, that he may be able by sound doctrine both to exhort and to convince the gainsayers.*

[10] *For there are many unruly and vain talkers and deceivers, specially they of the circumcision:*

[11] *Whose mouths must be stopped, who subvert whole houses, teaching things which they ought not, for filthy*

*lucre's sake.*
[16] *They profess that they know God; but in works they deny him, being abominable, and disobedient, and unto every good work reprobate.*

~ Titus 1:5-11,16


F rom this reading, we see that certain standards are expected of elders, leaders, or pastors who shepherd the flock and tend the husbandry of God. We are left in no doubt what the prerequisites and ongoing codes of practice are to qualify and stay qualified, what is required to take the reins of leadership amongst God's people. We see the standards of family life, personal life, and commitment to the work they are called to do, character traits and deficits that are unacceptable. We also see where the line must be drawn, and the microphone switched off to stop pastors speaking discordantly to the voice of the Spirit of grace and speaking words contrary to the Word of God.

Here lies the crux of my message to the many unruly and vain talkers and deceivers whose mouths, I suppose, ought to be stopped. I perceive that before God judges anyone, He will mercifully entreat them to repent. Paul says in Titus 1:13 – 'This witness is true. Wherefore rebuke them sharply, that they may be sound in the faith', likewise all who wish to see the salvation of souls and the reign of Christ in their lives, and in the body of Christ ought also to respond to and echo this admonition.

Repeatedly God is taken for granted because He is

slow to anger. However, when His pleas for us to turn around fall on deaf ears, He will step in and judge those who persist in this ecstatic rollercoaster ride of sin. He will terminate their sinful pleasures before many of those whom He sent His Son to pay an immense price for become eternally doomed. That time is now for some and near for others.

As our salvation is nearer than when we first believed, so is the time of judgement. Some choose to portray Christ as a cuddly baby in a manger or an extraordinarily loving and kind being who would not send anyone to an eternity of damnation for living contrary to His Word. How I wish that were the case, but it would mean we cannot take God at His Word on everything else He says in the Bible. I would rather believe the Word revealed in the Bible and make plans for eternity based on it! We should not be deceived by these lies of Satan to lull men into a false sense of security. Our God is a consuming fire, and like it says in the book of Hebrews, *"it is appointed unto men once to die, but after this the judgment."*

Earlier we read Apostle Paul's reference to a group of church leaders and how the motivation for their uncontrolled and vain talking is filthy lucre, or in more contemporary language, MONEY! Sadly, they caused so much damage to families, homes, and relationships that Paul demanded that their mouths be stopped. This evil phenomenon is no different from the ills perpetrated within the church today by some pastors and ministers of the gospel. According to the scripture, they have forsaken the right way and are gone astray, following the path of Balaam, the son of Bosor, who loved the wages of unrighteousness (2 Peter 2:15).

Now, do not get me wrong. We all make mistakes, and from time to time, we all displease God, but we ought to hastily make peace with God at such times. However, this is not the case with these folks as they are determined to persist in their ways, and like Balaam, despite repeated rebuke, do not know nor understand where to draw the line and turn back to the Good Shepherd for the redemption of their souls.

Notice that Paul alludes to the pre-eminence in their fleshly minds of their possession of the fleshly mark of circumcision. To my mind, this is indicative of, and congruent with, the concept of desiring men's approval by the ungodly yardstick of tangible earthly possessions, which have turned their hearts far away from God. These have set their affections not on things above but things on earth, contrary to the Word. They have also forgotten that a man's life does not consist of the abundance of things he possesses. Regrettably, some of them have passed on, and only Jehovah knows what has become of their souls. I would not speculate because the Word forbids that we judge anything before its time. However, I would hate for my loved ones to ever be in doubt as to where my soul might be upon my passing, should the Lord delay His coming.

Furthermore, in the following scripture, we see that this craze is not a 21st Century fad, but one which the Bible documents and is written for us upon whom the ends of the world have come.

*¹ But there were false prophets also among the people, even as there shall be false teachers among you, who privily shall bring in damnable heresies, even denying the Lord that bought them, and bring upon themselves swift destruction.*
*² And many shall follow their pernicious ways; by reason of whom the way of truth shall be evil spoken of.*
*³ And through covetousness shall they with feigned words make merchandise of you: whose judgment now of a long time lingereth not, and their damnation slumbereth not.*

~ 2 Peter 2:1-3

How can faithful saints not be pricked in their hearts if the way of truth is derided on their account?

Notably, the above verses refer to them as false teachers who come up with preposterous teachings that appeal to the unschooled in the Word and those with itchy ears that only want to hear what sounds melodious to their spiritually deaf ears. Thus, they make their hearer's common customers to whom they sell their feigned words for cash. The Word says their mouths must be stopped, and since the Word cannot fail, I urge the people of the Most High to relentlessly plead with God and invoke the power of God's Word, which shall not return to Him void, until we see their mouths stopped.

We have corroboration in another scripture concerning these self-serving pastors.

*¹⁵⁻¹⁶ God then said, "Dress up like a stupid shepherd. I'm going to install just such a shepherd in this land — a*

*shepherd indifferent to victims, who ignores the lost, abandons the injured, and disdains decent citizens. He'll only be in it for what he can get out of it, using and abusing any and all.*
¹⁷ *"Doom to you, useless shepherd,  walking off and leaving the sheep! A curse on your arm! A curse on your right eye! Your arm will hang limp and useless. Your right eye will go stone blind."*

~Zechariah 11:15-17 (MSG)

I pray with hope that these self-servants will sooner rather than later lose their strength and power base as they become exposed for who they truly are and lose insight as to how to deceive the people of God. Let these shepherds know that judgement is not far off; because the Chief Shepherd pronounces doom on them. Let every shepherd who is plying the craft of deception beware of the precarious nature of what he is doing. The Judge is at the door!

Also, we see these fearless fellows doing much harm to the people for whom the Son of God paid with His life. Hear this:

¹⁸ *Is it too little for you to have eaten up the good pasture, that you must tread down with your feet the residue of your pasture – and to have drunk of the clear waters, that you must foul the residue with your feet?*

~ Ezekiel 34:18 (NKJV)

These servants, of their own bellies, take what they can from God's people, and what they cannot take, they defile. They defile the flock's spiritual health and fellowship with God, through wanton disregard for the wholesome words of our Lord Jesus Christ, while spewing out the noisy rhetoric of what is at best a deceitful attempt at positive thinking laced with scripture-coated, motivational gibberish. Loud music and shouting are used to compensate for the absence of the Holy Ghost in their meetings, akin to the cavorting of people possessed with a spirit other than the One promised by the Father.

If you find yourself following shepherds such as these, I would advise you urgently and prayerfully seek the Lord to order your steps, and find another assembly of believers, for the sake of your soul. The Lord is at hand, and He will ask you to give an account. The responsibility for your eternal destination ultimately lies with you, and you alone!

I shall at once return to these stains in our midst, whom Jude refers to as...

*"...spots in your feasts of love, when they feast with you, feeding themselves without fear: clouds they are without water (no spiritual refreshing comes from them or their noisy words), carried about of winds (winds of every new doctrine or style of praying for, and preying on God's people); trees whose fruit withereth (to the extent that any new convert under their shepherding fails to thrive, how can they thrive without the very Word of Life?), without fruit (and so are left without fruit since their fruit cannot thrive), twice dead (stone dead, calloused hearts that are past feeling, having thoroughly seared their consciences),plucked up by the roots (they have become disconnected from the source of spiritual nutrition), raging waves of the sea, foaming*

*out their own shame, wandering stars, to whom is reserved the blackness of darkness forever."*

~ Jude 1:12-13

The state of these false teachers, pastors, and imposters will progressively deteriorate until they arrive at the place of reservation, an unenviable spot in the blackness of darkness forever. When Jesus lamented that not everyone that says to me Lord, Lord shall enter the kingdom of heaven, that they shall say we cast out demons in your name; and prophesied in your name, and you taught in our streets, and so on, do you suppose His pain was for the folks that had no connection to the church?

According to the scripture, these men had crept in unawares, just like the tares sown when men slept. They *"were before of old ordained to this condemnation, ungodly men, turning the grace of God to lasciviousness and denying the only Lord God and our Lord Jesus Christ"* (Jude 4). And some of these folks, who have sadly become infested with familiar spirits, mainly prophesy things that are familiar to people, offering mostly unnecessary bits of detailed information. Their prophecies have little instruction in righteousness but with a whole lot of attention and applause drawn to self. These, and the spirits motivating them, deny Jesus by failing to give Him the preeminent place, contrary to our understanding of the scripture that *"the testimony of Jesus is the Spirit of prophecy"* (Revelation 19:10).

Sadly, the dread of Jehovah has departed from these. Their sole objective is not sharing the pains of Jesus or filling up that which remains of His sufferings. They seek whatever gain they can get through Christ's name and the material offerings of His people. They do not visit the weak and poor of the flock, only the well to do who conduct themselves in open disobedience to the wholesome words of Jesus, and these pastors dare not rebuke such individuals! These impostors will be rebuked and exposed by the mercy and love of the Almighty to preserve His people for His kingdom and save His people to the uttermost. The option for deceivers and dubious pastors to repent remains available before Jehovah arises to contend with them.

> *[17] Because thou sayest, I am rich, and increased with goods, and have need of nothing; and knowest not that thou art wretched, and miserable, and poor, and blind, and naked:*
> *[18] I counsel thee to buy of me gold tried in the fire, that thou mayest be rich; and white raiment, that thou mayest be clothed, and that the shame of thy nakedness do not appear; and anoint thine eyes with eyesalve, that thou mayest see.*
> *[19] As many as I love, I rebuke and chasten: be zealous therefore, and repent.*
> *[20] Behold, I stand at the door, and knock: if any man hear my voice, and open the door, I will come in to him, and will sup with him, and he with me.*
>
> ~ Revelation 3:17-20

I exhort and implore these errant pastors that we measure ourselves by our need for, and the panting of our hearts after Jesus, and our desire to fellowship with and rely on Him. If that desire is absent, it indicates an urgent need to re-evaluate our place in Christ and what constitutes the object of our satisfaction. If our prized possessions are what constitutes the foundation of our satisfaction, then we ought to fear because the Word calls us wretched, miserable, poor, blind, and naked!

It is time to respond to the gentle and kind rebuke of the love of God. Open the door to Him. Start supping with Him and buy from Him true riches that shall not rot or rust, white garments to clothe our spirit bodies and use His prescribed eye drops, which is the enlightening by the Divine Spirit, to cure a lack of spiritual insight.

I will conclude with a reminder to those that choose to be obstinate; those who refuse and reject sound doctrine or adjudge themselves above God's Word and godly counsel:

> [4] *"Go through the streets of Jerusalem and put a mark on the forehead of everyone who is in anguish over the outrageous obscenities being done in the city."*
> [5-6] *I listened as he went on to address the executioners: "Follow him through the city and kill. Feel sorry for no one. Show no compassion. Kill old men and women, young men and women, mothers and children. But don't lay a hand on anyone with the mark. Start at my Temple."*
> *They started with the leaders in front of the Temple.*
> ~ Ezekiel 9:4-6 (MSG)

Remember, it is judgment time for we Christians; we are the first in line (1 Peter 4:17). Folks, we need to be sure that we bear the marks of our Lord Jesus.

As the Lord purges us of these deceivers, and as we walk holy before God, we shall thrive as never before, and yield more fruit until the angel cries to the One like unto the Son of man to thrust in the sickle to reap the earth. Maranatha!!

"...many high priests, or big-time ministers of our day, have forsaken the eternal Word of God and discarded the scripturally prescribed manner of serving the Lord."

# A MORE EXCELLENT WAY:
## The Love Construct

The book of First Corinthians chapter thirteen describes a more excellent way:

*¹ Though I speak with the tongues of men and of angels, and have not charity, I am become as sounding brass, or a tinkling cymbal.*
*² And though I have the gift of prophecy, and understand all mysteries, and all knowledge; and though I have all faith, so that I could remove mountains, and have not charity, I am nothing.*
*³ And though I bestow all my goods to feed the poor, and though I give my body to be burned, and have not charity, it profiteth me nothing.*
*⁴ Charity suffereth long, and is kind; charity envieth not; charity vaunteth not itself, is not puffed up,*
*⁵ Doth not behave itself unseemly, seeketh not her own,*

*is not easily provoked, thinketh no evil;*
*⁶ Rejoiceth not in iniquity, but rejoiceth in the truth;*
*⁷ Beareth all things, believeth all things, hopeth all things, endureth all things.*

~ 1 Corinthians 13:1-7

This more excellent way is the operating system of the Phinehas, son of Eleazer type priest. Love is the motivation for this type of priest or minister, a burning love towards God and the men to whom God has sent them.

First, we must establish what love is. There are two types of love; the love associated with or driven by our innate feelings and the love driven by the divine nature. The former is human-enabled, determined and propelled by our interactions with humans, while the latter is Spirit-enabled, determined and sustained by our interactions with the Spirit of God. This Spirit-enabled love is divine, and so are its manifestations and characteristics. The human-enabled love depends on interactions with the subject of that love and has a propensity to falter and fail. The Spirit generated and sustained love does not falter; it never fails. We find that the human-enabled love has a self-interest element while the Spirit-enabled love has a selfless element.

Therefore, a ministry of selfless love compared to a ministry of selfish love bears the hallmarks of Phinehas, son of Eleazar, and Phinehas, son of Eli ministries.

Who is at the centre of our care as ministers? The

interests of the people we are sent to serve or our own interests? Let us examine each Phinehas type ministry and identify the type of love that was manifest.

When the son of Eleazar took action, it was to please God and prevent his people's annihilation. He disregarded the probable consequences of his actions to himself. God first, others next is the philosophy of the kind of love the son of Eleazar demonstrates. The son of Eli thought of himself first and himself next. He showed no regard for God or the people he was supposed to be ministering to as a priest. This sort of love may appear to serve, but God does not regard such services. After all, the son of Eli went to serve in battle with the army of Israel. He probably put in a shift as a priest in the temple also!

The 1 Corinthians 13 Love passage tells us a lot about this concept: what love is and what it is not. You will find that it represents the son of Eleazar type of ministry. What it is not is a manifestation of the son of Eli type of ministry.

One is selfless love, while the other is self-centred love. One is divine, while the other is human. One is predicated on the power of the Spirit of God, and the other is motivated by ambition, personal interest or worse still, animated by a spirit other than the One promised by our Lord Jesus Christ, that sheds God's love abroad in our hearts.

So while Eleazar ministry types set their barometer by the attributes of verses 4-7, Eli type ministers are content with the flawed barometer of verses 1-3.

> ¹ *Though I speak with the tongues of men and of angels,*
> *but have not love, I have become sounding brass or a*
> *clanging cymbal.*
> ² *And though I have the gift of prophecy, and understand*
> *all mysteries and all knowledge, and though I have all*
> *faith, so that I could remove mountains, but have not*
> *love, I am nothing.*
> ³ *And though I bestow all my goods to feed the poor, and*
> *though I give my body to be burned, but have not love,*
> *it profits me nothing.*
>
> ~ I Corinthians 13:1-3 (NKJV)

Three attributes are evident from the preceding: irritatingly loud or noisy, nothingness and a lack of profitability or fruitlessness. Thus, despite the seemingly commendable activities of Phinehas, son of Eli type ministers, the absence of selfless love, initiated and sustained by walking in and with the Holy Spirit, negates and nullifies their supposedly laudable activities. This must be difficult to imagine because, as men, we look on the outside while God looks on the inside.

God does not reckon with man's evidence. He reckons with man's essence! This explains why He says, *"I know you not"* on judgment day, despite the seemingly compelling evidence presented by the Phinehas, son of Eli type ministers, about what they have done in His name. It is the alignment of our essence with God's essence by His Spirit's influence on our spirits that transforms us from Phinehas, son of Eli type ministers, to Phinehas, son of Eleazar type ministers, which implies that this problem can be fixed. Walking in the spirit is a learned experience in which we grow. Samuel, the prophet, learned it from Eli, but sadly Eli's son Phinehas refused to learn it from his own father.

These son of Eli type priests are obstinate, proud and unwilling to learn from others. They are unteachable, and they tend to be their own counsellors. They reject the scripture that teaches us that safety is in the multitude of counsellors, not as it relates to a specific matter (because that portends confusion rather than safety), but that through the course of a man's life and ministry, there is safety in learning from a multitude of people that God brings our way.

So back to walking in the Spirit; a demand of God by which we serve and worship Him acceptably as it is written:

> [23] *But the hour cometh and now is, when the true worshipers shall worship the Father in spirit and in truth;* **for the Father seeketh such to worship Him**
> ~ John 4:23

> [16] *So I say, walk by the Spirit,* **and you will not gratify the desires of the flesh.**
> ~ Galatians 5:16 (NIV)

> [6] *For to be carnally (externally or visible evidence) minded is death; but* **to be spiritually minded or inclined is LIFE AND PEACE.**
> ~ Romans 8:6

*<sup>25</sup> If we live in the Spirit, let us also **walk (keep step) in the Spirit**.*

~ Galatians 5:25

*<sup>8</sup> **The wind bloweth where it listeth and thou hearest the sound thereof**, but canst not tell whence it cometh, nor whither it goeth; **So is every one that is born of the Spirit**:*

~ John 3:8 (John Gill's Exposition of the Bible)

This birth mentioned in John 3:8 is determined and founded on the Word. Although the blowing wind causes the branches and foliage to sway back and forth after the rhythm of the Spirit, it does not move the tree from its foundation, the Word. Any wind that moves a person from their position in the Word is not of the divine Spirit. It is the false wind of every doctrine that tosses men to and fro. The Word, therefore, is the anchor of our spiritual walk. The divine Spirit will never sway us away from the confines of the Word. This, friends, is how we recognise true spiritual influences and leadings. This is what the son of Eli priests must set at the fore to learn for transformational influence by the Spirit of God.

In sharp contrast, the life of Phinehas, son of Eleazar priesthood, is characterised by the attributes we see highlighted in verses 4-7.

*<sup>4</sup> Love suffers long and is kind; love does not envy; love does not parade itself, is not puffed up;*
*<sup>5</sup> does not behave rudely, does not seek its own, is not provoked, thinks no evil;*
*<sup>6</sup> does not rejoice in iniquity, but rejoices in the truth;*

*⁷ bears all things, believes all things, hopes all things, endures all things.*

~ I Corinthians 13:4-7 (NKJV)

I must admit, and hopefully, so would you, that this is not the stuff of human capabilities. This can only be powered by divine machinery. Therefore, more likely than not, most of us will find that aspects of the preceding scripture will require a realignment in our lives to satisfy the demands of grace. This is the reason why God's plan and provision to deal with the difficulties we sometimes face when walking in His divine love comes in handy.

*³ And not only that, but we also glory in tribulations, knowing that tribulation produces perseverance;*
*⁴ and perseverance, character; and character, hope.*
*⁵ Now hope does not disappoint, because the love of God has been poured out in our hearts by the Holy Spirit who was given to us.*

~ Romans 5:3-5 (NKJV)

The Holy Spirit has copiously poured this divine love into our hearts, so we have it! Enough of it to prevent our hope from being disappointed as we encounter the 'niceties' of tribulations that work to reprogram our perseverance levels and thereby build our character. This is the type of character depicted in 1 Corinthians 13:4-7, which constitutes divine love attributes.

Now a Phinehas son of Eleazar priest ought to pray regularly that their *"love may abound yet more and more"* (Philippians 1:9) and also *"that you, being rooted and grounded in love"* (Ephesians 3:17 NKJV) to access the benefit of the gift of divine love copiously poured in our hearts by the Spirit of God. I believe that we ought to pray this for one another, especially for people we are called to work with because we are not ignorant of the devices of our enemy! We must relentlessly approach the throne of grace to obtain mercy and find grace to help in the moment of need (Hebrews 4:16) to walk as a Phinehas son of Eleazar priest! God, enable our march towards the realisation of selfless love in our ministries and priestly service.

We shall now explore some scriptures that practically show us how to walk this path, but we must remember that selfish objectives do not drive this type of priesthood. Phinehas, the son of Eleazar, was driven only by patriotic fervour for the nation of Israel. In the same way, we ought to be driven and consumed only by the zeal of the house of our God.

Jesus declared His patriotism:

> *¹⁶ And said unto them that sold doves, Take these things hence; make not my Father's house an house of merchandise.*
> *¹⁷ And his disciples remembered that it was written, The zeal of thine house hath eaten me up*
>
> ~ John 2:16-17

Jesus taught many new things that were, in fact, old teachings and principles but from a new and higher perspective. Take this for example:

> *²¹ Ye have heard that it was said of them of old time,*

*Thou shalt not kill; and whosoever shall kill shall be in danger of the judgment:*
*²² But I say unto you, That whosoever is angry with his brother without a cause shall be in danger of the judgment: and whosoever shall say to his brother, Raca, shall be in danger of the council: but whosoever shall say, Thou fool, shall be in danger of hell fire.*

~ Matthew 5:21-22

Jesus set the standard of love a couple of notches higher than what was prevalent at the time. This must be our reference point.

Of equal relevance and importance is the need to re-evaluate our understanding of the concept and practice of giving and receiving. Selfless love must be the driver of giving. Of course, Jesus taught on this subject extensively in the scriptures.

*⁶ He spake also this parable; A certain man had a fig tree planted in his vineyard; and he came and sought fruit thereon, and found none.*
*⁷ Then said he unto the dresser of his vineyard, Behold, these three years I come seeking fruit on this fig tree, and find none: cut it down; why cumbereth it the ground?*
*⁸ And he answering said unto him, Lord, let it alone this year also, till I shall dig about it, and dung it:*
*⁹ And if it bear fruit, well: and if not, then after that thou shalt cut it down.*

~ Luke 13:6-9

And from Isaiah 61, we can determine who the fig tree might allude to:

³ *To appoint unto them that mourn in Zion, to give unto them beauty for ashes, the oil of joy for mourning, the garment of praise for the spirit of heaviness; that they might be called trees of righteousness, the planting of the Lord, that he might be glorified.*

~ Isaiah 61:3

From these scriptures, we can conclude that the people of God must be in the frame regarding this unproductive tree. The wish to receive fruit from us is the ultimate expectation of God, and the best gift we can give back is to be fruit yielding plants of the Lord. Remember, Jesus said that, *"except a corn of wheat fall down and die, it abides alone..."* This is the ultimate gift we can give to God. Jesus Himself showed us the perfect example by 'bringing many sons to glory' Hebrews 2:10.

Interestingly, we do not see any example of Jesus bringing money to the temple, though He clearly teaches the principle and endorsed it. However, we see him canvassing daily for souls as He said, *"I must do the works of Him that sent me while it is day for the night comes when no man can work"*.

In a nutshell, the higher standard of giving is the gift of souls. This expectation is so important that the husbandman declares that enough is enough regarding the fruitless tree, telling them to cut the tree down as it was only taking from the ground and yielding nothing in return. So, just like the fig tree, we have continually made the ground of truth on which we stand, and upon which we are planted, of no effect by yielding no fruit for the vine owner. But hang on, there is good news.

The vinedresser, the Holy Ghost, makes intercession for us and promises to dig around and dung us so we can become productive. Praise God for the Holy Ghost, who is our Helper.

Thus, the higher standard of giving is soul-winning, and a pleasing gift that we can offer to God is the souls of men, women and children. Remember, the ones promised a chance to shine as the stars are those that win souls. To this higher level, God is calling us today, and I believe it is the ultimate demonstration of our love to God first and our neighbours next!

———— ❧ ⬥ ☙ ————

"The Spirit generated and sustained love does not falter; it never fails."

———— ❧ ⬥ ☙ ————

# PURSUING AN ABUNDANT ENTRANCE

We all want to do well and enjoy a copious experience of the Kingdom of God as well as finish our course well and eventually receive an abundant entrance into the Kingdom of God. I have considered the sort of entrance Elijah received when the heavenly 'Limousine Service' of chariots and horses of fire took him home. The pearly gates must have been thrown wide open for the grand entrance. Ours may not be a 'Limo Service', but it can still be one that accords us an abundant or rich entrance!

*⁵. And beside this, giving all diligence, add to your faith virtue; and to virtue knowledge;*
*⁶. And to knowledge temperance; and to temperance patience; and to patience godliness;*
*⁷. And to godliness brotherly kindness; and to brotherly*

*kindness charity.*

*[8]. For if these things be in you, and abound, they make you that ye shall neither be barren nor unfruitful in the knowledge of our Lord Jesus Christ.*

*[9]. But he that lacketh these things is blind, and cannot see afar off, and hath forgotten that he was purged from his old sins.*

*[10]. Wherefore the rather, brethren, give diligence to make your calling and election sure: for if ye do these things, ye shall never fall:*

*[11]. For so an entrance shall be ministered unto you abundantly into the everlasting kingdom of our Lord and Saviour Jesus Christ.*

~ 2 Peter 1:5-11

We have learned that Phinehas, the son of Eleazar, our ministry example, was approved by God. The attributes that set him apart for approval by God are worth summarising and emulating.

## Acknowledgement of our status and pursuit of repentance

Our collective and individual statuses need to be acknowledged. Where am I in relation to where God wants me to be? Similarly, where are we as a people in relation to the expectation of God? This is crucial to any progression with God. We must acknowledge our position, determine how that relates to God"s ideals and expectations and promptly set ourselves right if we are not where we ought to be. In a nutshell, self-appraisal and an evaluation of our collective status done sincerely will result in a change of course back to God. This is what Phinehas, the son of Eleazar, demonstrated and exemplified.

*31. For if we would judge ourselves, we should not be judged.*

~ 1 Corinthians 11:31

*5. Examine yourselves to see if your faith is genuine. Test yourselves. Surely you know that Jesus Christ is among you; if not, you have failed the test of genuine faith.*

~ 2 Corinthians 13:5 NLT

In this regard, an openness to help from materials, friends and most importantly accepting conviction and responding to the workings of the Holy Spirit upon our hearts are expedient.

## Setting Landmarks

*28. Remove not the ancient landmark, which thy fathers have set.*

~ Proverbs 22:28

Phinehas, son of Eleazar, was concerned that the landmark set for the children of Israel by the ancients was being relocated by the likes of Zimri. He understood the Word that admonishes us not to remove the old landmark set by our progenitors. Now, for us today, the landmarks set or the boundaries set are those set by the Word. Consequently, we must seek to follow the Word as the pointer to those set landmarks and pray for their rooting in our lives; (the blessings of abiding within the set landmarks and the consequences of not will no doubt become evident). So, regular self-appraisal would be helpful to keep us within the boundaries of the landmarks set by precepts from the Word by our fathers in the faith and by their abiding examples. In so doing, we become setters of landmarks for our children in the faith. This admonition is reiterated in 2 Timothy 2:2 and similarly in 1 Timothy 4:12:

> [2]. *And the things that thou hast heard of me among many witnesses, the same commit thou to faithful men, who shall be able to teach others also.*
>
> ~ Timothy 2:2
>
> [12]. *Let no man despise thy youth; but be thou an example of the believers, in word, in conversation, in charity, in spirit, in faith, in purity.*
>
> ~ 1 Timothy 4:12

Thus a regular review of our spiritual status would be a responsible endeavour to ensure we do not slip away from the landmarks set by the Word. E. W. Kenyon said he would often ask his colleagues in the faith if they had perceived spiritual growth in his life in the months before. To him, spiritual growth, like physical growth, must be perceptible by those closest to us.

## The Spirit of the Fear of the Lord

Praying for the fear of the Lord over our lives is necessary to achieve the Phinehas, son of Eleazar persona. This attribute is not only alluded to in the Old Testament:

> [3]. *and he will delight in the fear of the Lord. He will not*

*judge by what he sees with his eyes, or decide by what he hears with his ears;*

~ Isaiah 11:3 (NIV)

But also in the New Testament:

*[31]. Then the church throughout Judea, Galilee and Samaria enjoyed a time of peace and was strengthened. Living in the fear of the Lord and encouraged by the Holy Spirit, it increased in numbers.*

~ Acts 9:31 (NIV)

*[1]. Therefore, since we have these promises, dear friends, let us purify ourselves from everything that contaminates body and spirit, perfecting holiness out of reverence for God.*

~ 2 Corinthians 7:1 (NIV)

*[21]. Submitting yourselves one to another in the fear of God.*

~ Ephesians 5:21

# Walking in the Love of the Lord

Adding to our prayer for the fear of God is the need to pray for the shedding abroad of God's love in our hearts by the Holy Spirit, and that "we abound yet more and more in love."

Romans 5:5 says, *"And hope maketh not ashamed; because the love of God is shed abroad in our hearts by the Holy Ghost which is given unto us."* In Ephesians 3:17-19 and Philippians 1:9, these Pauline prayers demonstrate the importance of faithfully making this request recurrently to the Father of our Lord Jesus Christ. We also know that the Word tells us in 2 Thessalonians 3:5:

> *5. And the Lord direct your hearts into the love of God, and into the patient waiting for Christ.*
>
> ~ 2 Thessalonians 3:5

We can ask that He direct our hearts into love of Him. Remember the two sons sent to the field? While one promised to go but did not, the other, who refused to go initially, went. Jesus then asked rhetorically which of these two sons did his father's will. Evidently, the yardstick of approval by God for having fulfilled His purposes is not lip promise but active obedience. The Lord said, "If you love me keep my commandments." This attribute of love toward God is paramount.

## Under Divine Influence

Phinehas, son of Eleazar, clearly had his motivations from a higher influence than the other Phinehas, son of Eli. God (and His Word or precepts) was his Motivator! In the New Testament, we would say he was "Looking to Jesus the author and finisher of his faith." *(Hebrews 12:2)*

Phinehas could read and tell the mind of God. This is evident because he got God's approval after his swift action against Zimri and Cozbi. Again, in the light of the New Testament, he, like Jesus, was "Doing what he saw the Father do." He was undoubtedly contending for the faith once accorded to the saints:

his uncle Moses and dad Aaron! *(Jude 3-5)*

His approval by the Almighty God made him a figure worthy of emulation. He became an "example of the believer" *(1 Timothy 4:12)*. This is a key attribute that we must strive for in all our striving for excellence as servants who must give account for our works on earth.

So let us examine Acts 20:18-33, which typifies the modus operandi of Phinehas, son Eleazar type ministers.

*18. And when they were come to him, he said unto them, Ye know, from the first day that I came into Asia, after what manner I have been with you at all seasons,*

*19. Serving the Lord with all humility of mind, and with many tears, and temptations, which befell me by the lying in wait of the Jews:*

*20. And how I kept back nothing that was profitable unto you, but have shewed you, and have taught you publickly, and from house to house,*

*21. Testifying both to the Jews, and also to the Greeks, repentance toward God, and faith toward our Lord Jesus Christ.*

*22. And now, behold, I go bound in the spirit unto Jerusalem, not knowing the things that shall befall me there:*

*23. Save that the Holy Ghost witnesseth in every city, saying that bonds and afflictions abide me.*

*24 But none of these things move me, neither count I my life dear unto myself, so that I might finish my course with joy, and the ministry, which I have received of the Lord Jesus, to testify the gospel of the grace of God.*

*²⁵. And now, behold, I know that ye all, among whom I have gone preaching the kingdom of God, shall see my face no more.*

*²⁶. Wherefore I take you to record this day, that I am pure from the blood of all men.*

*²⁷. For I have not shunned to declare unto you all the counsel of God.*

*²⁸. Take heed therefore unto yourselves, and to all the flock, over the which the Holy Ghost hath made you overseers, to feed the church of God, which he hath purchased with his own blood.*

*²⁹. For I know this, that after my departing shall grievous wolves enter in among you, not sparing the flock.*

*³⁰. Also of your own selves shall men arise, speaking perverse things, to draw away disciples after them.*

*³¹. Therefore watch, and remember, that by the space of three years I ceased not to warn every one night and day with tears.*

*³². And now, brethren, I commend you to God, and to the word of his grace, which is able to build you up, and to give you an inheritance among all them which are sanctified.*

*³³. I have coveted no man's silver, or gold, or apparel.*

~ Acts 20:18-33

It is necessary to highlight some valuable characteristics of the sort of minister or priest we should emulate from the foregoing scripture.

**i.** Stay focused on our given objectives despite opposition from folks who should know better or from our background. This will include others who proclaim knowledge of God.

**ii.** Keep working and keep pushing the objective, the sound gospel of repentance and faith.

**iii.** Don't be moved, don't be perturbed, don't alter course to satisfy or to please anyone but God. Aim to finish your ministry with the joy of accomplishing your given tasks.

**iv.** Aim to be free from the blood of anyone who chooses death over life by not failing to give them opportunities to hear the truth and counsel of God.

**v.** Feed and nurture God's people so they can defend themselves from false teachers and prophets in your absence.

**vi.** Reiterate the reality of the hope and the damnation that the gospel teaches. *(See 2 Peter 3:1).*

**vii.** Avoid setting our sights on the money and material possessions of our flock or anyone associating with us or visiting our ministries. This singular evil act was the cause of the destruction of Achan and his household and the defeat as well as the setting back of God"s people. *(See Joshua 22:20)*

## Identification of faithful men and women

*². And the things that thou hast heard of me among many witnesses, the same commit thou to faithful men, who shall be able to teach others also.*

~ 2 Timothy 2:2

As Phinehas, the son of Eleazar-type ministers, we

must be eager to identify faithful men and women who we know will follow the same pathway. Like Samuel, the prophet of old, we ought to rely on God to help us identify such persons. We must be careful not to lay hands on or endorse anyone hastily to avoid giving a platform to wolves in sheep"s clothing who will scatter the flock and tear some asunder. Having made this mistake, I can assuredly say that it sets back your ministry.

Note that with the sons of Eli, the ministry line from Eli was truncated, the baton was passed to unfaithful ones. In their case, it was a race into oblivion. We must ensure the ministry committed to us is not run into oblivion either as a result of failing to commit things we have learned from the Holy Spirit to faithful men or because we commit things to unfaithful men. Worse still is the damage of committing things that God has not taught us to others to propagate.

## Our Sender is our Appraiser and Approver

We, in the mould of the son of Eleazar, must both resist and desist from the applause and approval of men. God, our Sender, must be the One to whom we return for appraisal and approval. As an example, God had this to say about Phinehas, the son of Eleazar:

> [11]. *Phinehas, the son of Eleazar, the son of Aaron the priest, hath turned my wrath away from the children of Israel, while he was zealous for my sake among them, that I consumed not the children of Israel in my*

*jealousy.*

~ Numbers 25:11

Also, Jesus, the scripture says, was approved of God.

²². *Ye men of Israel, hear these words; Jesus of Nazareth, a man approved of God among you by miracles and wonders and signs, which God did by him in the midst of you, as ye yourselves also know:*

~ Acts 2:22

We also learn of Apelles as approved in Christ (Romans 2:22), while 2 Corinthians 10:18 (NKJV) says, "For not he that commends himself is approved, but whom the Lord commends."

Charles Spurgeon taught his students never to ask their hearers for an assessment of their sermons but to go to God instead for that appraisal. He reasoned that a bad review could result in dejection while a good review could result in pride! With God, a bad review will be swiftly followed by the encouragement of the Holy Spirit, and a good review will be to a good and faithful servant, meaning you know your place as a mere servant. So, to God we must go!

## All-Consuming Zeal

This approved son of Eleazar was approved only because, as the earlier scripture in Numbers 25 reads, "he was zealous for my sake among them." This all-consuming zeal earned him recognition with the Most High and Jealous God and a blessing of peace and everlasting priesthood to him and his descendants!

> *12. Wherefore say, Behold, I give unto him my covenant of peace:*
> *13. And he shall have it, and his seed after him, even the covenant of an everlasting priesthood; because he was zealous for his God, and made an atonement for the children of Israel.*
> ~ Numbers 25:12-13

On the strength of this scripture and knowing that God cannot lie, we may conclude with certainty that somewhere on the earth, descendants of this Phinehas are ministry gifts today and enjoying God's peace in their lives. Hallelujah!! Then to further buttress my conviction of the necessity of this attribute, we see our Lord and Saviour, Jesus Christ, declare that the passion of God's house has consumed Him when the purpose of the house of God was being subverted, abused and misappropriated for personal gain by money changers.

> *15. Jesus made a whip from some ropes and chased them all out of the Temple. He drove out the sheep and cattle, scattered the money changers" coins over the floor, and turned over their tables.*
> *16. Then, going over to the people who sold doves, he told them, "Get these things out of here. Stop turning my Father"s house into a marketplace!"*
> *17. Then his disciples remembered this prophecy from the Scriptures: "Passion for God"s house will consume me."*
> ~ John 2:15-17 (NLT)

# Cutting off offensive tendencies

*⁴². And whosoever shall offend one of these little ones that believe in me, it is better for him that a millstone were hanged about his neck, and he were cast into the sea.*

*⁴³. And if thy hand offend thee, cut it off: it is better for thee to enter into life maimed, than having two hands to go into hell, into the fire that never shall be quenched:*

*⁴⁴. Where their worm dieth not, and the fire is not quenched.*

*⁴⁵. And if thy foot offend thee, cut it off: it is better for thee to enter halt into life, than having two feet to be cast into hell, into the fire that never shall be quenched:*

*⁴⁶. Where their worm dieth not, and the fire is not quenched.*

*⁴⁷. And if thine eye offend thee, pluck it out: it is better for thee to enter into the kingdom of God with one eye, than having two eyes to be cast into hell fire:*

*⁴⁸. Where their worm dieth not, and the fire is not quenched.*

~ Mark 9:42-48

This passage of scripture teaches a few avenues of offence, from which we are admonished to desist.

First is offence against the young of the flock of Christ over which we are overseers. We learn from Hebrews 13:17 that we shall give account for them! We also learn the fate of the servant that causes offence to the little ones of the flock of God in Mark 9:42, referenced above. So our priesthood requires a commitment to the flock, to nurture and protect the flock of Christ, not tripping them up and enticing them to sin.

Second, on this fearful list of offences is the hand in verse 43. The hand is suggestive of our work, as is evident in the Word. *(See Deuteronomy 2:7 and Psalm 90:17)*

> [7]. *For the Lord thy God hath blessed thee in all the works of thy hand: he knoweth thy walking through this great wilderness: these forty years the Lord thy God hath been with thee; thou hast lacked nothing.*
>
> ~ Deuteronomy 2:7

> [17]. *And let the beauty of the Lord our God be upon us: and establish thou the work of our hands upon us; yea, the work of our hands establish thou it.*
>
> ~ Psalm 90:17

So, if our work causes us offence or to stumble and sin, we are commanded to let go of it; cut it off.

Next is the foot, which denotes our pathway and direction. See the Word declares in Psalm 1:1, "Blessed is the man that walketh not in the counsel of the ungodly, nor standeth in the way of sinners, nor sitteth in the seat of the scornful." Before the man sits or takes residence in "Scorn City", he first begins his journey walking in ungodly counsel. Then he stands in the way or lifestyle of sinners. The journey of waywardness to the place of residing in sin is what our Lord demands that we truncate or cut off.

And then there is the eye which is suggestive of our focus. We learn that a focus of the eyes on the desires of the eyes is of the world and not the Father.

*16. For everything in the world — the lust of the flesh, the lust of the eyes, and the pride of life - comes not from the Father but from the world.*

~ 1 John 2:16 (NIV)

This scripture essentially encapsulates the offences of our handiwork being the pride of life, our waywardness being the lust of the flesh and our decadent focus being the lust of the eyes.

## Link up with like-minded folk, but leave room to extricate yourself from corruption

Christian service is not intended as a solo endeavour or venture. In the New Testament, we see ample reference to the Body of Christ.

*16. From whom the whole body fitly joined together and compacted by that which every joint supplieth, according to the effectual working in the measure of every part, maketh increase of the body unto the edifying of itself in love.*

~ Ephesians 4:16

*21. In whom all the building fitly framed together groweth unto a holy temple in the Lord:*

~ Ephesians 2:21

The operative word in these two passages is FITLY, which means to render close-jointed together or to organise compactly. There is a sense from these scriptures that we support and feed off each other for our edification or growth. While we are encouraged to do this, we are also advised to remove or extricate ourselves from folks who reject and deviate from the wholesome words of the Lord Jesus (not those unable to appropriate their New Creation truths to their lifestyles).

> *3. If any man teach otherwise, and consent not to wholesome words, even the words of our Lord Jesus Christ, and to the doctrine which is according to godliness;*
> *4. He is proud, knowing nothing, but doting about questions and strifes of words, whereof cometh envy, strife, railings, evil surmisings,*
> *5. Perverse disputings of men of corrupt minds, and destitute of the truth, supposing that gain is godliness: from such withdraw thyself.*
>
> ~ 1 Timothy 6:3-5

Furthermore, it is notable that the scripture admonishes as follows:

> *6. Your glorying is not good. Know ye not that a little leaven leaveneth the whole lump?*
>
> ~ 1 Corinthians 5:6

> *33. Be not deceived: evil communications corrupt good manners.*
>
> ~ 1 Corinthians 15:33

We must therefore be careful to avoid condoning attitudes that frustrate the grace of God. As a classic biblical example, the dissimulation or pretentious behaviour of Peter and Barnabas was called out by Paul; otherwise the grace of God on the lives of the Gentile believers could have been frustrated. *(See Galatians 2:12-14)*

# Motivating Not Comparing

These two attitudes are on opposite ends in scripture.

> *12. For we dare not make ourselves of the number, or compare ourselves with some that commend themselves: but they measuring themselves by themselves, and comparing themselves among themselves, are not wise.*
> ~ 2 Corinthians 10:12

Clearly, from this scripture, comparison demonstrates a lack of wisdom and results in the disapproval of God. Comparison is driven not by a desire to please God but by a desire to impress people. Nadab and Abihu fell victim to this lack of wisdom and disapproval of God. They, along with their works, were rejected and judged harshly by God. They determined in their hearts and carried out their plot to falsely attribute to God a manifestation of fire which was of their own making so they could appear as priests whose worship and sacrifice were approved of God. God called it a strange fire because it did not come from His throne. They overlooked the truth that the Lord knows them that are His, and for everyone that calls on His name to depart from iniquity. These older sons of Eleazar most probably wanted to demonstrate to the people, certainly not to God, that they had the approval of God like their younger brother Phinehas. They strayed into the realm of comparing themselves with Phinehas, and this lack of wisdom resulted in summary rejection! Many priests or ministers have strayed into the place of staging manifestations as though from God to obtain the approval, acknowledgement and following of men. This is dangerous territory.

On the flip side is the God-approved approach, which is to MOTIVATE ONE ANOTHER.

> *24*. *Let us think of ways to motivate one another to acts of love and good works.*
> *25*. *And let us not neglect our meeting together, as some people do, but encourage one another, especially now that the day of his return is drawing near.*
> ~ Hebrews 10:24-25 (NLT)

This is characterised by collaboration between the motivator and the motivated. You encourage others to do what you do and guide them in the process. This amounts to mentoring others to do what God has taught you. It creates room for others to walk the path you walk, teaching them the things you have learned. The ministry, modelled after Phinehas, son of Eleazar type of priesthood, is not about hoarding knowledge, experience and manifestations of the Spirit. Instead, it is about looking out for faithful men equally committed to passing the torch of the Christ-Life to other faithful ones. And so, on and on and on. How intriguing that we see this concept fulfilled in God"s promise to Phinehas, son of Eleazar, when He said in

> *12*. *Now tell him that I am making my special covenant of peace with him.*
> *13*. *In this covenant, I give him and his descendants a permanent right to the priesthood, for in his zeal for me, his God, he purified the people of Israel, making them right with me."*
> ~ Numbers 25:12-13 (NLT)

This Phinehas, son of Eleazar, indeed is a dependable model of service in priesthood and ministry.

"Where am I in relation to where
God wants me to be?"

# STAND UP FOR JESUS

As we draw the curtain on this evaluation of contemporary priesthoods, let us examine a few more verses of scripture.

> 30 Then stood up Phinehas, and executed judgment: and so the plague was stayed.
> 31 And that was counted unto him for righteousness unto all generations for evermore.
>
> ~ Psalm 106:30-31

> 1 Now after these things, in the reign of Artaxerxes king of Persia, Ezra the son of Seraiah, the son of Azariah, the son of Hilkiah,
> 2 The son of Shallum, the son of Zadok, the son of Ahitub,
> 3 The son of Amariah, the son of Azariah, the son of

*Meraioth,*
*⁴ The son of Zerahiah, the son of Uzzi, the son of Bukki,*
*⁵ The son of Abishua, the son of Phinehas, the son of Eleazar, the son of Aaron the chief priest:*
*⁶ This Ezra went up from Babylon; and he was a ready scribe in the law of Moses, which the Lord God of Israel had given: and the king granted him all his request, according to the hand of the Lord his God upon him.*

~ Ezra 7:1-6

From the preceding scriptures, we see several interesting and salient points. First, that God observed and honoured the son of Eleazar for his pursuit of righteousness as well as God's ideals and standards as revealed to the children of Israel at that time. Secondly, down the line, his descendant Ezra was again called upon by God to pursue and fulfil another godly assignment.

God remembers the Phinehas that pursued His ideals but makes no further mention of the Phinehas who pursued his personal desires. He forgot Phinehas, the son of Eli, but remembered Phinehas, the son of Eleazar.

God takes a serious view of sin and the bearers of sin. The case of Phinehas, the son of Eli, has been written as an example for us to consider. After fathering Ichabod and his untimely demise by death, we hear no more of this son of Belial. This archetypical priest of the departure of the glory had hope only in this life and died a miserable, pitiful fellow. Modern-day Ichabodian priests and ministers will have their fill in this world, but like their prototype, avoidable misery shall sadly be their end.

Conversely, God commends the son of Eleazar after his death. Indeed, *'the memory of the just is blessed, but the name of the wicked shall rot.'* (Proverbs 10:7).

Let us imagine for a moment that as unregenerate men, we all bear on our backs a sin backpack. As soon as we confess our faults to God, this backpack is detached, taken away, discarded, and we are cleansed from the after-effects of this sin. However, for sin not confessed, the backpack grows bigger, is heavier and smells worse while remaining affixed to the back of the bearer. In light of this, let us have a look at 1 Timothy:

> [24] *Some men's sins are open beforehand, going before to judgment; and some men they follow after.*
>
> ~ 1 Timothy 5:24

(Please note the words *'follow after'* mean to accompany in the original Greek word - *epakoloutheo*)

At this juncture, we must stress how crucial the timing of the appearance of our sins before God is.

For some, their sins are open, not concealed. Their sins are confessed early and sent ahead to attend judgement before them. For others, their sins accompany them to judgement because they are unconfessed and concealed. This is a dreadful position to be in.

God will promptly, consistently, and decisively deal

with sin that appears before Him. He will assign sins going before (preceding in time and space) to judgement to the annals of His forgetfulness before the individuals who have committed those sins turn up for judgement, totally sin-free by the sacrifice of Jesus. On the other hand, those who hold on to their sins, and permit those sins to follow them to judgement will, along with their sins, be removed from the presence of God.

The eternal sacrifice of the Lord Jesus permits us to send our sins beforehand to judgement before we turn up for judgement. That holy sacrifice deals with our sins before the Father.

Therefore, it would seem extremely unwise for any of us to persist in sin and disregard all warnings and pleas to return to the ways prescribed by the Lord. I plead with priests after the order of Phinehas, son of Eli, to understand the risk they take by persisting in the way they go and turn back to the Father. Turn back to His ways, means and methods; His plans and purposes; and run with them and pursue their fulfilment. This brethren is the only way to usher His presence and power into our churches, ministries and communities, and lead men to an eternity with Him who gave His life for us.

Remember, we have an assurance that God will forgive our sins, and that He will abundantly pardon us:

> [12] *As far as the east is from the west, so far hath he removed our transgressions from us.*
>
> ~ Psalm 103:12

*¹⁷ And their sins and iniquities will I remember no more.*

~ Hebrews 10:17

*⁴ Blessed is the man whom thou choosest, and causest to approach unto thee, that he may dwell in thy courts: we shall be satisfied with the goodness of thy house, even of thy holy temple.*
*⁵ By terrible things in righteousness wilt thou answer us, O God of our salvation; who art the confidence of all the ends of the earth, and of them that are afar off upon the sea:*

~ Psalm 65:4-5

This teaches and confirms to us what we later read in 1 Peter 2:

*⁹ But you are a chosen people, a royal priesthood, a holy nation, God's special possession, that you may declare the praises of him who called you out of darkness into his wonderful light.*

~ 1 Peter 2:9 (NIV)

We are a chosen people, and what a blessing that is! We are privileged to come into His presence to minister to Him, having been called a royal priesthood. So, it is essential that we identify with this honourable priesthood and avoid the tendencies of the son of Eli priesthood. As we do this, we will witness the manifestation of His righteousness and show forth, publish, make known and celebrate His praises.

Everything else has failed and will fail. It is

incumbent on our generation to hasten to bring back the King, but we must first turn to Him, walk with Him, and be enabled to work for Him. Then we can honestly say, "Come, Lord Jesus, come."

> [19] Not a blacksmith could be found in the whole land of Israel, because the Philistines had said, "Otherwise the Hebrews will make swords or spears!"
> [20] So all Israel went down to the Philistines to have their plow points, mattocks, axes and sickles sharpened.
> [21] The price was two-thirds of a shekel for sharpening plow points and mattocks, and a third of a shekel for sharpening forks and axes and for repointing goads.
> [22] So on the day of the battle not a soldier with Saul and Jonathan had a sword or spear in his hand; only Saul and his son Jonathan had them.
> ~1 Samuel 13:19-22 (NIV)

The foregoing has, in a sense, befallen the church. We have outsourced the shaping and sharpening of our tools of warfare to those who fail to put the Word first. Unfortunately, they have refused to sharpen our weapons of war (swords and spears) after the pattern of the Word. Instead, they limit the sharpening of our tools to those for servicing our mundane needs (mattocks, forks, axes and goads) at an extortionate price. In fact, because they so often oppose the Word, the Body and Bride of Christ finds herself in a place where it is without sufficient blacksmiths, wordsmiths in our ranks who rightly divide the Word!

We can no longer continue to outsource the sharpening of our weapons of warfare to the sons of Eli. In these times, every committed pastor and servant of God must take up the active service of sharpening the tools of warfare. By speaking the truth of the Word in season and out of season, by actively encouraging other saints and believers, by often speaking to one another and refuting the baseless teachings of the Ichabodian priesthood that happens to be prevalent and very vocal.

It is incumbent on you, my brothers and sisters, to no longer hold your peace but instead shout from the rooftops what the Lord is ministering to you in your closets. Let us make the all-important choice to join the ranks of the priesthood of Phinehas the son of Eleazar because it is written:

> *35 And I will raise me up a faithful priest, that shall do according to that which is in my heart and in my mind: and I will build him a sure house; and he shall walk before mine anointed for ever.*
>
> ~ 1 Samuel 2:35 (ASV)

May God bring the platforms of the sons of Eleazar type priests together that we may, in the unity of the Spirit, deliver His Word to our generation!

Stand up, stand up for Jesus,
Ye soldiers of the cross;
Lift high his royal banner,
It must not suffer loss.
From victory unto victory
His army shall he lead,
Till every foe is vanquished,
And Christ is Lord indeed.


Stand up, stand up for Jesus,
Stand in his strength alone;
The arm of flesh will fail you,
Ye dare not trust your own.
Put on the gospel armor,
Each piece put on with prayer;
Where duty calls or danger,
Be never wanting there.

# EPILOGUE
## ~ Seeker's Prayer ~

*[19]. Change your hearts and lives! Turn back to God so that your sins may be wiped away.*
*[20]. Then the Lord will provide a season of relief from the distress of this age and he will send Jesus, whom he handpicked to be your Christ.*

~ Acts 3:19-20 (CEB)

*[3-4]. Most important, know this: in the last days scoffers will come, jeering, living by their own cravings, and saying, "Where is the promise of his coming? After all, nothing has changed – not since the beginning of creation, nor even since the ancestors died."*
*[9]. The Lord isn't slow to keep his promise, as some think of slowness, but he is patient toward you, not wanting anyone to perish but all to change their hearts and lives.*

~ 2 Peter 3:3-4, 9 (CEB)

Lord God, my heart is hardened; please make it soft and yielding. Cleanse me of my sins as I repent of my waywardness. Restore to me the joy of Your salvation. Give, I pray, a new spirit within me, a spirit of love for You, fear of You and a fresh desire for You. Change me, and help me put the Word (Jesus) first in my life.

Help me, Lord. Help me serve You acceptably with reverence and godly fear, and help me serve my generation in all your will in Jesus' name, I pray. Amen.

# AN ODE
## GIVEN IN THE SPIRIT OF PROPHECY
### by Pastor Emiko Amotsuka
### on December 31st, 1999
*(with permission)*

There is a new faith in the land. It is different from that into which I was born through the sacrifice of Christ.

In the old faith into which I was born, Jesus Christ, the son of the Living God, is the centre of attraction. He is the subject of worship. All hearts bow to him. In the new faith, the man of God, not Jesus, is the centre of attraction. The "man of God" is the subject of adoration. He is adored for the power that exudes from him, not the power to change men from sinners to saints, but the power that is evidenced by the money he has behind him and the crowd that gathers to listen to him.

Yes, there are testimonies of miracles from the

people, but in these testimonies, Jesus of Nazareth is not the star of the story. It is the man of God, the father in the Lord, who prays; he gets the glory.

There is a new faith in the Land. Outwardly, it resembles the old faith into which I was born through the sacrifice of Jesus Christ, but it takes a discerning eye to see that it is not quite the same.

In the old faith, the messenger is a broken vessel through whom Christ is portrayed. In the new faith, the man of God is so visible; I can hardly see Christ. How can I see Christ when the man of God captivates my attention with stories of his millions, of his exotic houses and cars, the names of the high and mighty who have come  to him for prayer, and the size and the exploits of the ministry that far surpasses what any other ministry will ever dream of.

There is so much to admire and adore in the man of God that you can hardly think of the man of Galilee. Yet, it is only that humble Galilean, Jesus Christ, that has the power to change lives and bring real and lasting peace and joy, but the powerful man of God has stolen the show.

Oh, man of God, will you not retrace your steps to Calvary and hide behind the cross so that the world can see Jesus Christ, the true Giver of Life. For until we commit ourselves to portray Christ, and Christ alone, churches may multiply, but evil will persist and grow in the land, for though men gather in churches, it is not to meet Christ but to meet the anointed man of God.

Jesus said, *"and I, if I be lifted up from the earth, will draw all men unto me"* (John 12:32) and Paul said, *"not I, but Christ"* (Galatians 2:20).

# ABOUT THE AUTHOR

Ernest Hale Akwenuke was the convener of the 'Word Assembly', a series of regional camp meetings for University students and fresh graduates.

He currently leads an assembly of believers at the New Life Church, Emerson Park, in the United Kingdom.

Ernest is married to Wola and the father of Joel and Samuel.